Immigrants in
& Selected Early Poems

ALSO BY JIMMY SANTIAGO BACA

Black Mesa Poems

Martín & Meditations on the South Valley
Introduction by Denise Levertov

Jimmy Santiago Baca

Immigrants in Our Own Land & Selected Early Poems

A NEW DIRECTIONS BOOK

Grateful acknowledgments are made to the editors of the books and chapbooks in which the poems in this volume originally appeared: *Fired Up With You!* (Border Publishing Company, 1977), *Immigrants in Our Own Land* (Louisiana State University Press, 1979), *New Directions in Prose and Poetry 38* (New Direc-tions, 1979), *Swords of Darkness* (Mango Publications, 1981), and *What's Happen-ing* (Curbstone Press, 1982).

Manufactured in the United States of America
New Directions Books are printed on acid-free paper.
Published simultaneously in Canada by Penguin Books Canada Limited
First published as New Directions Paperbook 701 in 1990

Library of Congress Cataloging-in-Publication Data
Baca, Jimmy Santiago, 1952–
  Immigrants in our own land & selected early poems / Jimmy Santiago Baca.
    p. cm.
  ISBN 0-8112-1145-2 (NDP701 : alk. paper) : $8.95
  I. Title.
PS3552.A254I48   1990   90-6444
811'.54—dc20   CIP

New Directions Books are published for James Laughlin
by New Directions Publishing Corporation,
80 Eighth Avenue, New York 10011

SECOND PRINTING

Contents

Immigrants in Our Own Land

Selected Early Poems

Immigrants in Our Own Land
& Selected Early Poems

The Sun on Those

The sun on those green palm trees, lining
the entry road to prison. Stiff rows of husky-scaled bark,
with a tuft of green looping blades on top, sword twirling
in wind, always erect and disciplined, legallike.
Cars glide through the rows, like white swans
on summer afternoons. The assistant warden in a government car
is passed through the check point, in his new shirt and silk socks,
and silent hum of engine, a well-ordered life of favor for favor,
getting him where he is, on that road between palm trees,
soft hands, and ears seldom hearing screams and eyes never
the blood of these cellblocks, bucketfuls weekly, taken
to the slop pen, along with broken ribs, cutoff fingers
caught in doors of cages, often, dead men thrown to the hoofed mud
like chewed corn husks. He goes on softly on new tires, pressing
gas pedal, feeling the comfortable tug of speed taking him
from the never ending stillness of prison, from the thing
that never changes, made of rock and steel, moving like
a river down the days. King of this river, power to let some
drown or swim, river god on wheels, to a café downtown now,
to meet a woman and have dinner.
My father used to plant trees around fields
to protect crops. Trees against the wind, growing like me
in my father's eyes, budding out, trees spreading out, leaves
holding up their hands to protect the alfalfa and corn. We
would pass the trees, and he would point to them; all that
he owned was those trees. While men hounded him, took his land,
none knew about his trees; in jail cell after jail cell,
those trees were his secret. I was not his only son. And when
they captured me through the turn of my days, one was still
free, greening more, spreading wide in wind, sheltering crows,
and mourning our imprisonment, rejoicing our endurance, ever
plunging its roots deeper into the face of progress and land-
grabbers. Fences mean nothing to the trees.
Walls and fences cannot take me away from who I am, and I
know, as the tree knows, where I come from, who is my father.

I Will Remain

To Tello Hinojosa (xinoxosa)

I don't want to leave any more or get transferred
        to another prison because this one is too tough.
I am after a path you cannot find by looking at green fields,
        smelling high mountain air that is clear and sweetly
Odorous as when you fall in love again and again and again.
I am looking for a path that weaves through rock
        and swims through despair with fins of wisdom.
A wisdom to see me through this nightmare,
        not by running from it; by staying to deal blow for blow.
I will take the strength I need from me,
        not from fields or new friends. With my old friends
        fighting!
Bleeding! Calling me crazy! And never getting the respect I desire,
        fighting for each inch of it. . . .
I am not one of those beautiful people,
        but one of the old ones, a commoner of the world
You can find in taverns, seaports carrying bamboo baskets with fish,
        drinking coffee in a donut shop, weeping in the dark
In a two-for-five ramshackle hotel room,
        dreaming and walking along a city street at dawn.
To move about more freely, to meet and talk with new people,
        to have silence once in a while, to live in peace,
Without harassment of cops pulling you in as a suspect,
        these are very beautiful thoughts.
But I will remain here where the air is old and heavy, where life is grimy,
Full of hate at times, where opportunities are rare,
        anger and frustration abundant,
Here in this wretched place I most wish to leave
        I will remain.
I stay because I believe I will find something,
        something beautiful and astounding awaits my pleasure,
Something in the air I breathe,
        that will make all my terrors and pains seem raindrops
On a rose in summer, its head tilted in the heat
        as I do mine.
Here on this island of death and violence,
        I must find peace and love in myself, eventually freedom,
And if I am blessed, then perhaps a little wisdom.
I stay here searching for gold and ivory in the breast of each man.
I search for the tiny glimmering grains in smiles and words
        of the dying, of the young so old old, of the broken ones.

Count-time

Everybody to sleep the guard symbolizes
on his late night tour of the tombs.
When he leaves, after counting still bodies
wrapped in white sheets, when he goes,

the bodies slowly move, in solitary ritual,
counting lost days, mountng memories,
numbering like sand grains
the winds drag over high mountains
to their lonely deaths; like elephants
they go bury themselves
under dreamlike waterfalls,
in the silence.

The Handsome World

The handsome, broad-shouldered world, with
its great blue eyes, its thrashing and vigorous veins, its
rough hands fit for anything, turning, and its legs blocking
up the sky, giant world I live in, your tremendous embrace,
your uncombed hair during the workday, or at night, you
stand erect and glittering, escorting the most beautiful
women, and under the lights, I stand wondering if you are
a god, if other gods in their starry thrones lean forward
from their sleepy edens, to ponder on your growing arms,
your fuller voice, your looking up to them, and in your
eyes, a slight spark of renegade war, cries and shines
defiantly.

It's all well, husky barrel-chested cities
of America. Drowning in your liquor and gambling and clothes,
your rebels and libraries, your blood vessels filled and gorged
as if dams broke loose and hurtled toward gutters and gulches,
none can stop you, all rush to their boats made of bone,
and sails made of red cloth from the heart, and sail you America,
waving to others, all passing, passing and floating by.

So in all your grand wonder and greatness,
I wonder, who am I here? And thinking of this, I feel like
driftwood, knocked and banked on any shore, grabbed by any
hand up high, carrying its weight, and I beneath, bubbling
for life, for each breath.

Then I said, I will prove I am someone.
I dropped what I was doing, and left with nothing but me.
Well, now, this is all I am, breathing with firm eye toward
the distance. Ah, how lovely, how happy I am to be just me.
I raise my pink gums like a wild chimpanzee, tilt my head back,
chortling white-toothed, at this amazing zoo and its visitors,
pockets filled with popcorn, and crunching candy apples,
I just laugh and jump down the road . . . walking all day, free
of my leash.

So this is who I am? The world a playground
of steel bars and merry-go-rounds? But you see the sun up
there? You see the sky, and how it drips with rain like old
rafters, and from its corners birds swoop out and dive, you
see this land, the uniformity against cruel angry mountains,
I see it all; the glare of chrome and glaze of windows,
the suspense and ambition of young boys playing baseball
in parks, and sidewalks splattered with the night's blood,

4

and the policeman sleeping with his wife and farting in
the bathroom, and then after, so groomed and polished,
passing shops along the street, hello he says to one,
hello to another. I sleep in the grass thinking of this,
and can be arrested for sleeping on the grass, and I laugh
looking at the sky, filling the sky with my laughter,
the treetops bend and birds scatter out.

        I stand up, grass all around me, and start
walking through the tall grass, listening to myself live,
hearing my foot lift and set, lift and set, carrying me
like a stray animal, a holy one who rose out of mud, with mind
of man, heart of earth, taking my body-form as others,
from now on, I scream and howl and love and laugh, I am me.

It's Going To Be a Cold Winter

A batch of new guards, trained to sniff out
brittle tip-ends of straw brooms, packed into my cell
this morning.

Door barely open; like a sleepy slave on the
run, sweating on a cotton mattress, my eyes open frightened,
then aware, and focusing on solid faces, summer-burned red,
I crawl out of bed.

I stand up: one pats my legs, the pads of my
hard feet, runs his hands beneath my balls, over my penis,
up along my ribs, under my armpits, in my ear fingers dig,
through my hair they crawl, and then, like cargo tied and
wound up with suspicious eyes, I am placed aside.

They enter my cell: a legal pillow fight
begins with my books and papers. Stir crazy madmen, papers
sidling down to cement floor, my mattress turned over, sheets
torn away like a mask hiding tons of heroin; but nothing,
only cotton, cheap sweaty moldy-smelling cotton, picked by
slaves, sewed up by slaves, slaves of the Greater State,
that come in all colors.

My books are leafed through, I imagine,
hound dogs howling up a tree at some paragraph of wild bird
or squirrel. They ravish up my poems in folders, their eyes
scan the blood and misery I write about that is here, the
disrespect for our human bodies and emotions, they lick
with long steady tongues, on the other side of my experience,
a badge between us, like a door as tall and guarded as any
of heaven's for rebuking sinners.

I can see their teeth and their eyes. Some-
thing greater holds them in tow, and human words cannot
pull them away. Something drives them to do what they are doing.
It's not gold anymore, as it was with their fathers, it's
them, so small, they fit themselves among fraternities
of terror, growing suddenly, losing their place as humans,
to become polished boots and black club dangling from belts.

They laugh like home boys loving mom's apple
pie. Good American men. Behind their shades (they all wear
sunglasses), their eyes turn gray, and I imagine some ghostly
farmer as their souls, holding up an ancient rifle, saying,
"Atta boy, Atta boy. Get em boy, dadgumit, get em!" and
the guards, ever quickly scrambling through my belongings.

Bankers seat themselves before dark-red rich
oak desks. New fresh dresses are put on by women. Breakfast
scents drape the morning air. School children giggle, pass
through shortcuts to school, while the earth almost seems
to soften their passage, sprinkling dew about, dogs to run,
trees to swoosh their leaves, young lovers to smile with the
moon's mellow lips. Healthy workers enjoying coffee, talking
trade stuff, and utility bills. Streets adorned with shops,
and people gesturing with hands, and doors shutting, and
the bulky growl of cars sputtering up for a spin around
the block to pick up some lard, flour, sugar, and eggs,
at the corner grocery.
        And I'm standing here in my boxer shorts,
my hair like bozo the clown, my soul a gigantic tent, filled
with the circus of life, the elephants sounding, and the
escaped tigers bursting from my cage, to tell me, "Okay. We're done."

Ancestor

It was a time when they were afraid of him.
My father, a bare man, a gypsy, a horse
with broken knees no one would shoot.
Then again, he was like the orange tree,
and young women plucked from him sweet fruit.
To meet him, you must be in the right place,
even his sons and daughter, we wondered
where was papa now and what was he doing.
He held the mystique of travelers
that pass your backyard and disappear into the trees.
Then, when you follow, you find nothing,
not a stir, not a twig displaced from its bough.
And then he would appear one night.
Half covered in shadows and half in light,
his voice quiet, absorbing our unspoken thoughts.
When his hands lay on the table at breakfast,
they were hands that had not fixed our crumbling home,
hands that had not taken us into them
and the fingers did not gently rub along our lips.
They were hands of a gypsy that filled our home
with love and safety, for a moment;
with all the shambles of boards and empty stomachs,
they filled us because of the love in them.
Beyond the ordinary love, beyond the coordinated life,
beyond the sponging of broken hearts,
came the untimely word, the fallen smile, the quiet tear,
that made us grow up quick and romantic.
Papa gave us something: when we paused from work,
my sister fourteen years old working the cotton fields,
my brother and I running like deer,
we would pause, because we had a papa no one could catch,
who spoke when he spoke and bragged and drank,
he bragged about us: he did not say we were smart,
nor did he say we were strong and were going to be rich someday.
He said we were good. He held us up to the world for it to see,
three children that were good, who understood love in a quiet way,
who owned nothing but calloused hands and true freedom,
and that is how he made us: he offered us to the wind,
to the mountains, to the skies of autumn and spring.
He said, "Here are my children! Care for them!"
And he left again, going somewhere like a child

8

with a warrior's heart, nothing could stop him.
My grandmother would look at him for a long time,
and then she woud say nothing.
She chose to remain silent, praying each night,
guiding down like a root in the heart of earth,
clutching sunlight and rains to her ancient breast.
And I am the blossom of many nights.
A threefold blossom: my sister is as she is,
my brother is as he is, and I am as I am.
Through sacred ceremony of living, daily living,
arose three distinct hopes, three loves,
out of the long felt nights and days of yesterday.

I Am Sure of It

Just after supper sheets were passed out,
the sheets smell clean as I make my bed,
warm from the laundry dryers and soft.
I spread the first sheet over my mattress,
smooth it out and tuck it in.
"32581 . . ." I look back up and there's a guard.
"32581 . . ." and I nod affirmatively.
He leaves the letter on the bars and goes on.

It's from a magazine I sent three poems to.
On the envelope in bold black letters,
it's rubber-stamped, FUNDS RECEIVED . . . AMOUNT $10.
I open the letter and read the first paragraph.
They usually don't pay for poems, they say,
but wanted to send a little money in this case,
to help me out. My poems were beautiful,
and would be published soon.

Holding this letter in my hand,
standing in the middle of my cell,
in my boxer shorts, it's now, times like this,
rapt in my own unutterable surprise, I wonder about people . . .
I take a few steps to the toilet and pull myself up,
my mouth on the back grill at the back of my cell,
just about to holler down to my buddy in another cell,
when I am struck silent by the window across from me,
and look outside, upon a few convicts at dusk,
running in pairs around the baseball diamond,
or some close to the fence that separates them from freedom,
they walk, pointing arms to freedom.
The grass is green, trees lulled in deep spring slumber,
sun going down at the west edge of earth.

Shadows cover hovering sunrays, shaking sun out of leaves.
boughs dark, fields darken perceptibly, leaving
one solitary walker, hands jammed in coat pockets,
looking down with a blue beenie cap over his head, thinking,
thinking, as he walks around the field one last time, then disappears.
The baseball diamond is empty now.
The smell of cool spring is in the night air, above all things,
and toy-sized cars crawl in black distances,
headlights roving into long roads of darkness,

leaving small towns behind, sparkling in streetlamps,
a single car slides into a great wave of darkness,
a nightworker, searching stars and breathing fresh air,
the hum of engine and whir of wheels,
drone on in the silence of a Tuesday night.
Grass crickets tune their fiddles on the wind;
by rumbling trucks on the freeways,
construction workers coming and going into homey bars,
greasy caps cocked to one side, smoking cigarettes,
stroking pool cues through gritty thick fingers,
suck their unbrushed teeth watching intently,
as Tammy Wynette wails out her country hits
to dimes and quarters plunked in the jukebox,
among the bearish beer-drinking, smoke-swirling workers,
coughing and cursing and smiling,
while their fathers push on screen doors,
enter yellowed kitchens and drink coffee with married daughters,
as night darkens over the city
and porch lights collect bugs in their nets . . . .

All the while we convicts live in a smooth block of rock,
convicts scan through their TV guides,
and through all the different blubbering channels,
an old Mexican song floats out from someone's cell,
recalling memories; under the screams and gunshots
tumbling out of TVs, memories float heavy in me,
and I think of tennis shoes my grandfather
bought for me as a child for my birthday.

My life so filled with simple things!
With beds and people crying and laughing and fighting,
towns and voices and kisses and unforgettable nights,
walking on sidewalks or through grass at dusk,
this is life, I am sure of it. . . .
I step down from the toilet, grab the sheet and tuck it in.
I spread the blanket over, then sit down,
thinking all the time, this is life,
even in prison, respecting each other, helping each other,
close or far away, it doesn't matter, I am sure of it.

Immigrants in Our Own Land

We are born with dreams in our hearts,
looking for better days ahead.
At the gates we are given new papers,
our old clothes are taken
and we are given overalls like mechanics wear.
We are given shots and doctors ask questions.
Then we gather in another room
where counselors orient us to the new land
we will now live in. We take tests.
Some of us were craftsmen in the old world,
good with our hands and proud of our work.
Others were good with their heads.
They used common sense like scholars
use glasses and books to reach the world.
But most of us didn't finish high school.

The old men who have lived here stare at us,
from deep disturbed eyes, sulking, retreated.
We pass them as they stand around idle,
leaning on shovels and rakes or against walls.
Our expectations are high: in the old world,
they talked about rehabilitation,
about being able to finish school,
and learning an extra good trade.
But right away we are sent to work as dishwashers,
to work in fields for three cents an hour.
The administration says this is temporary
So we go about our business, blacks with blacks,
poor whites with poor whites,
chicanos and indians by themselves.
The administration says this is right,
no mixing of cultures, let them stay apart,
like in the old neighborhoods we came from.

We came here to get away from false promises,
from dictators in our neighborhoods,
who wore blue suits and broke our doors down
when they wanted, arrested us when they felt like,
swinging clubs and shooting guns as they pleased.
But it's no different here. It's all concentrated.

The doctors don't care, our bodies decay,
our minds deteriorate, we learn nothing of value.
Our lives don't get better, we go down quick.

My cell is crisscrossed with laundry lines,
my T-shirts, boxer shorts, socks and pants are drying.
Just like it used to be in my neighborhood:
from all the tenements laundry hung window to window.
Across the way Joey is sticking his hands
through the bars to hand Felipé a cigarette,
men are hollering back and forth cell to cell,
saying their sinks don't work,
or somebody downstairs hollers angrily
about a toilet overflowing,
or that the heaters don't work.

I ask Coyote next door to shoot me over
a little more soap to finish my laundry.
I look down and see new immigrants coming in,
mattresses rolled up and on their shoulders,
new haircuts and brogan boots,
looking around, each with a dream in their heart,
thinking they'll get a chance to change their lives.

But in the end, some will just sit around
talking about how good the old world was.
Some of the younger ones will become gangsters.
Some will die and others will go on living
without a soul, a future, or a reason to live.
Some will make it out of here with hate in their eyes,
but so very few make it out of here as human
as they came in, they leave wondering what good they are now
as they look at their hands so long away from their tools,
as they look at themselves, so long gone from their families,
so long gone from life itself, so many things have changed.

The County Jail

Men late at night cook coffee in rusty cans,
just like in the hills, like in their childhoods,
without rules or guidance or authority, their fathers
dead or wild as gypsies,
their mothers going down for five dollars.
These are the men who surface at night,
The sons of faceless parents,
the sons of brutal days dripping blood,
the men whose faces emerge from shadows,
from bars,
and they join in circles and squat on haunches,
share smokes, and talk of who knows who,
what towns they passed through;
while flames jump under the coffee can,
you see new faces and old ones,
the young eyes scared and the old eyes
tarnished like peeling boat hulls,
like wild creatures they meet,
with a sixth sense inside of them, to tell them
who's real and who's the game;
and their thoughts are hard as wisdom teeth,
biting into each new eye,
that shows itself around the fire.

The coffee is poured steaming hot into cups,
and the men slowly sip.
Shower stalls drip bleakly in the dark,
and the smell of dumb metal is inflamed
with the acrid silence, and once in a while,
a car horn will sound from outside the windows,
and the man with only a cheek illuminated by the fire,
the rest of his face drenched in shadows,
will get up and leave the circle,
return to his bunk.

Summary

In the morning I throw water over my face,
do about fifty push-ups to wake me up;
put my jeans and T-shirt on,
make myself a cup of coffee in a can,
brewed with wads of toilet paper
on the floor of my cell, to boiling,
then poured into my cup;
then I sit on my bunk, improvise a few books
as a desk, and write a letter.

The cell doors are racked open: time to go to work.
Field crews on the athletic field unravel warm hoses,
water gurgles out bubbly white. A warm breeze
yawns over the tawny grass, dry, stiff, crunchy.

Inside the walls, main-yard crews
gather up shriveled leaves, crumbling flowers, scrape
cracked bits of twigs, hot powder on their brogan boots,
rattling their twangy garden rakes,
                    across rock hard dirt.

Chain gangs line up outside, load themselves into white trucks,
past the main gate, and sitting on benches in back,
we pass the warden's daughter on the curb,
under a tree with her two nephews;
the ice-cream truck audible a block away,
ding-a-ling ding-a-ling;
even she sweats in the crotch today,
leaving a thirst in us all.

The fields we pass alongside the road
froth with pungent odors, juices in roots and leaves
evaporate in shimmering heat waves.
The cane fields gasp their splintered stalks,
the pale horizon drawn up behind us
like the ending of an old picture show
about bad guys who made the world pause a moment,
before getting trampled under, kicked out,
and the world going on with the business at hand.

We turn into a weed-choked path, exhaust pipe sputtering,
tires grinding against weeds and dust,
all of us in the back bouncing and bumping shoulders,

15

sweating, feeling good about the rough ride,
about looking out the back of the truck to the road,
leading to memories, to things we never talk about.

The truck stops in a cloud of hot dust.
We jump out and start cleaning ditches, pulling weeds,
take our shirts off, and set our feet squarely in the dirt.

Stony, Fifteen Years in the Joint

Fifteen years in the joint . . .
He knows his way around this place,
Bulletproof eyes,
Body tough as metal,
A neatly folded handkerchief
Hanging out of his back pocket
Like a presidential car
He walks slowly across the compound
Waving at cons standing
On cellblock landings,
With a smile
That is just part of the rules.

Like an Animal

Behind the smooth texture
Of my eyes, way inside me,
A part of me has died:
I move my bloody fingernails
Across it, hard as a blackboard,
Run my fingers along it,
The chalk white scars
That say I AM SCARED,
Scared of what might become
Of me, the real me,
Behind these prison walls.

When Life

Is cut close, blades and bones,
And the stench of sewers is everywhere,
Blood-sloshed floors,
And guards count the dead
With the blink of an eyelid, then hurry home
To supper and love, what saves us
From going mad is to carry a vacant stare,
And a quiet half-dead dream.

Jewelry Store

After work, when supper lights and slippers
come on, when traffic dims, and those remaining look up
from their car and truck windows to the gray clouds
marbly pockets piled up, slowing, slipping down,
light, purple rain gently clawing, so gently sprinkling . . .

I wonder which ring I should buy, if
I buy one. Their brightness storms even worse,
diamonds, bracelets, necklaces, all around this table
watching me, old kings, queens, stabled for sale.

I can hear laughter of old knights and virgins
sparkle from them, the yellow teeth of the king smile at me
from a ring, rubied in wine of the night.

I appear here before you all, with a heart.
I've come to buy you, take you to my woman, a little woman
insignificant to the world but to me, I buy all your land
and stock that glitters from you, I make you my serfs, slaves,

Black rings, white diamonds, you will sit
like shepherds among the folds of hair of my woman, or
along her wrist, you can yearn upon her hands as you might
your laden chest of gold,

Look to her bosom and lips, when at night
we sleep, and you all, glittering as you would in moonlight,
try to unclasp yourselves. . . .

In the window, cars pass swishing through
puddles. I had forgotten the age I live in. Still thinking
of this, still looking in the window, to the building across
the street, I imagined a field just blessed with rain,
and the people of this town coming toward the field,
each with something he's sewed, or cooked, or made of wood,
the black people with their beads placed upon my first child's breast,
and Spanish music starts up, stirring leaves, we clap,
big husky white men laugh up a wind . . . I feel the fresh smell
of wood, and the leaf crying its fresh green . . .

On that ring.

The city lights slowly peep on the wet street.
Soggy smell in the air gray, and the smell of grass damned near
drowns me in its love. I walk down the street.

Joe

They just brought us breakfast. My celly wakes up
　　And we talk and eat.
His wife went to a fortune-teller
　　And according to her he will be getting out soon.
He is a Vietnam vet doing time on a junk beef.
　　He gives me coffee and cigarettes
And I compose poems for his wife and two young girls.
　　He is a loner with big brown eyes.
He combs his light brown hair in the morning
　　And I taunt him jovially about his farts.
I think the American troops evacuated Nam because of his farts.
　　He is a blue ribbon winner in the sport
Of passing air. He shares everything with me,
　　Soap, pants, shirts, coffee and cigarettes.
And what food I don't want on my tray I give to him.
　　His philosophy is simple: just let me and my family
Live in peace. A Chicano who picked cotton when young,
　　Wisps caught in his hair
On afternoons when he visited his girl,
　　Then married her and worked as a meatcutter;
His wife gave birth to a baby girl, then they adopted another one,
　　Then off to Vietnam to serve a country
Whose heels only he had seen. . . .
　　And when back, all it could offer him was prison,
Breakage of love bonds between him and his family,
　　Sunken cheeks and eyes turning pale
Like a great bear in hibernation during Spring,
　　Streams rot black, berries shrivel, and the sound
Of gunfire in the distance,
　　Tractors plowing under his life
As he watches from those great pale eyes,
　　Tractor blades claw his heart out,
Remove it slowly like a great mountain, drilling a tunnel
　　Right down the middle of it,
Dynamiting it, as his dreams tumble down into heaps of rubble.
　　But still, he wakes up this morning,
Is a porter for our tier, giving out trays, hustling
　　Up and down stairwells.
Losing so much, Big Joe, house, car, horses,
　　Your daughters weeping for your presence,

Your wife your only bridge to reality,
    Where do you go from here, Big Joe?
Denver, California, or will you stick around Arizona?
    You with no friends, only acquaintances,
With an old army suit hanging in your closet back home,
    With you banging against the door of Hope
Until your knuckles bleed,
    Diving into your memories hitting rock bottom,
Blood trickles from your eyes,
    The burnt stubs of church candles.
Even if you say you have only acquaintances,
    And blindfold yourself from closer ties,
In the dusty square of town we have never been to
    I buy you a beer and read you a poem
And stand at your side if ever you need me.

In My Land

Time gets lost. You see it
like the spurt of a match in the night, and then it is
suddenly blotted out black under the sun.
The old people remember yesterday, the women
when their skirts got wet crossing the streams, the men
wood smoke in their hair and sap of piñon trees on their hands.
But you look up, and where grandfather's guns
used to hang, now books stand, their pages yellowed.
A dog howls outside
at red evening. The windmill creaks. The mud is fresh
with cow hooves. There is a broken-down bus, and among weeds,
rusty frames of 32s and wooden plow handles, and a grave
or two with paper flowers pink and withered, rain stained.

In this land there is a graveness, of color
and heart. Here the white sands cannot absorb the rich blood
that sun sponges light from.
Here wounds open in the heart like cracks
in a mountainside, here there is a solitude in each person,
like a cave where a portion of the person sits and thinks.

Cattle move lazily to troughs. You cannot
put a price on a land where grass burns a green fire
that blinded my heart when young, and now gives it sight.
You cannot shout down the voice of water,
when over parched clay it whispers,
licking its wounded children of roots.

The cities here have grown large. When you
visit a girl, watch out for your muddy boots on the carpet.
And if you smell like sheep and coyote you better wash,
for the city will not understand you.

There is a TV in every house. And when you
sit there, waiting to take out your girl, the wind from the window
will give you strength to change, or meet the change.

There is college, and parties, and neighborhoods
with old wood and whistling boys, and people will cross
cultural barriers, holding up their arms protecting what little
they own, some will drown from their innocence,
And blackest hair ever will flag wildly
in the breeze, you will believe nothing so beautiful has ever been,
And as myself, you will be born again and again,
in this land, to carry the pain of change, the courage of love,
like the mountain over the valley, we must have the courage
of love, to live.

So Mexicans Are Taking Jobs from Americans

O Yes? Do they come on horses
with rifles, and say,

                    Ese gringo, gimmee your job?

And do you, gringo, take off your ring,
drop your wallet into a blanket
spread over the ground, and walk away?

I hear Mexicans are taking your jobs away.
Do they sneak into town at night,
and as you're walking home with a whore,
do they mug you, a knife at your throat,
saying, I want your job?

Even on TV, an asthmatic leader
crawls turtle heavy, leaning on an assistant,
and from a nest of wrinkles on his face,
a tongue paddles through flashing waves
of lightbulbs, of cameramen, rasping
"They're taking our jobs away."

Well, I've gone about trying to find them,
asking just where the hell are these fighters.

The rifles I hear sound in the night
are white farmers shooting blacks and browns
whose ribs I see jutting out
and starving children,
I see the poor marching for a little work,
I see small white farmers selling out
to clean-suited farmers living in New York,
who've never been on a farm,
don't know the look of a hoof or the smell
of a woman's body bending all day long in fields.

I see this, and I hear only a few people
got all the money in this world, the rest
count their pennies to buy bread and butter.

Below that cool green sea of money,
millions and millions of people fight to live,
search for pearls in the darkest depths
of their dreams, hold their breath for years
trying to cross poverty to just having something.

The children are dead already. We are killing them,
that is what America should be saying;
on TV, in the streets, in offices, should be saying,
   "We aren't giving the children a chance to live."

   Mexicans are taking our jobs, they say instead.
   What they really say is, let them die,
   and the children too.

To Come Live with Me

Was my wish. How funny that I didn't think
how we would make it. Looking at my face, asking the questions,
to see my expression. You looked long enough, at your mother,
laboring over steam kettles, the same faded dress on. You
looked longer at your father. . . .
It was my wish that you come with me. It was
not love: for in the superstitious deeps of myself, there was
a fear, I was afraid. There was lust, I wanted your body. There
was loneliness.
And you still carried yourself, a little
parochial schoolgirl, in your hands, as if a little creature
uncaged from your science class, you brought yourself home,
one day, and knew your womanly instincts.

How would we live? If not on love,
but the sting and hook of dreams, square under our round hearts,
how would we live, my Innocence?

And that is why, when songs came on the radio,
we'd close our eyes sometimes, and listen to them, chiseling
the square softer, into make-believe moments we never had.

So when we kissed, it was the tiger and rabbit
scenting their flesh paths around a tree. The fur of your heart
I would claw to smithereens, with tufts at lips thick-heavy.
You in my stomach, my dark eyes flickering light,

but no love. And like a tiger I strode down
long night streets in rain, unable to sleep, a lone figure,
across dead hulky sleep of parked cars, among walks of buildings,
shortcuts through fields, to the middle class of clustered homes,
swallowed in a blue dark.

How well we knew we didn't love. You came to me
because my shoulders were this wide, my jaw set so, and smile
on your eye. You came too quick, sandy to my legs, then waist,
and to me, my face, your tongue wrapping mine, and I trying
to catch my breath.

And you never told me, and that was agony.
And I never knew, and this was double agony, active as breath
and sleep for young bodies.

I'll no longer dream of setting stars down
at your feet like white rocks, cooled by my breath, for you to walk.
I'll no longer dream mountains less strong than I, and lighter
than you. No longer will I be silent for fear of the words
that might come.

But like stubs of a henchman's legs climbing
the burnt land of dreams, I will be normal like the rest. None
see my gnarled legs, the burnt land, behind my snow-cold blue veins
where one remembers the lust of youth as love so warm. . . .

The New Warden

He sat in the cool morning.
He had a handful of seeds in his palm.
He sat there contemplating
Where he would plant them.
A month later he tore the kitchen down
And planted apple seeds there.
Some of the convicts asked him why:
"Apples," he said, "is one of America's
great traditional prides. Remember
the famous ballad Johnny Apple Seed?"
Nobody had heard of it, so he set up
A poetry workshop where the death house had been.
The chair was burned in a great ceremony.
Some of the Indian convicts performed
Ancient rituals for the souls of those executed in the past.
He sold most of the bricks and built
Little ovens in the earth with the rest.
The hospital was destroyed except for one new wing
To keep the especially infirm aged ones.
And funny thing, no one was ever sick.
The warden said something about freedom being the greatest cure
For any and all ailments. He was right.
The cellblocks were razed to the ground.
Some of the steel was kept and a blacksmith shop went up.
With the extra bricks the warden purchased
Tents, farming implements and bought a big yellow bus.
The adjoining fields flowed rich with tomatoes, pumpkins,
Potatoes, corn, chili, alfalfa, cucumbers.
From the nearby town of Florence, and as far away as Las Cruces,
People came to buy up loads and loads of vegetables.
In one section of the compound the artists painted
Easter and Christmas and other holiday cards, on paper
Previously used for disciplinary reports.
The government even commissioned some of the convicts
To design patriotic emblems.
A little group of engineers, plumbers, electricians
Began building solar heating systems and sold them
To elementary schools way under cost. Then,
Some citizens grew interested. Some high school kids
Were invited to learn about it, and soon,
Solar systems were being installed in the community.

An agricultural program opened up.
Unruly convicts were shipped out to another prison.
After the first year, the new warden installed ballot boxes.
A radio and TV shop opened. Some of the convicts' sons
And daughters came into prison to learn from their fathers'
Trades and talking with them about life.
This led to several groups opening up sessions dealing with
Language, logic, and delving into past myths and customs.
Blacks, Mejicanos, Whites, all had so much to offer.
They were invited to speak at the nearby university
Discussing what they found to be untouched by past historians.
Each day six groups of convicts went into the community,
Working for the aged and infirmed.
One old convict ended up marrying the governor's mother.

In the Desert

                    In the desert there is a rain
that burns deeper than the heat.
                    Its blue flames drip down every root,
glisten every spare lean leaf in brilliance.
                    The rocks turn redder,
                    the dirt and sand darker,
a dog howls in short short barks, and spins wildly
                    after his tail, which leads
                    to a frog-jump jump,
and nighthawks whirl on white-tipped wings against coming night,
                    and the light breeze
will glow across the night, chanting hey hey hey softly,
                    the trees with their warped guitar branches
lament a love in their thirsty faces,
                    when in the desert it rains.

                    My friends are scattered around here.
Their natures different as rock and cliff, a small rock
you can pick up in your hands,
                    a cliff that drowns you with the wrong step,
friends, my friends are scattered at corners like fires
                    I stand before, asking no questions,
                    in the night in the desert when it rains.
                    True, rain gives life here. It gathers
the deepest parts of your hidden hardness in you,
                    and dissolves it for you to drink,
                    in the desert.

                    There are no days in the desert. They may be,
but they slip razor-sharp by me, like doors for the entering rain,
                    Its train I hold in the drops in my hands,
                    its passing over the land,
                    a ghost fuller than any human flesh
                    among the bones
                    in the desert.

The Painters

The painters paint over my shoes,
over my heart, over my face,
their brushes sweep across,
across, trying to blend me in
with everything else.

In gluey clumsiness,
the moon unsticks itself and rises
leaving a trail of yellow footsteps,
through the soot and grime.
Bells drip blue iron notes
down the streets,
and the wind sticks to tree branches,
heavy with smog,
like wet bristles of a brush
dipped in black paint;
the dumb hardened boughs
ladder up splinteringly
scraping the sky.
Chipped leaves peel off
and beat themselves
on dull dark doors of the city.

With the acrid-smelling stuff
of my soul,
I rub the roots and
I rub and rub,
and slowly the old burnish
of an autumn leaf draws out,
roots begin to move,
and I hold a fistful of earth
in my palm,
and accept my uniqueness,
my exile, from the painters.

Sleeping Convicts in the Cellblock

They dream the sun rising above carved cliffs,
Dawn's transparent nets of mist
Float over the stone,
And stars breathe their last dim flames
Into the crystal pure air of twilight.
The whole prison is asleep.
A lone songbird alights on the windowsill
With outspread wings,
In beautiful halo of widening dawnlight;
When the clang and grind of steel doors is silent,
It sings to the new day,
Its wings beckoning for flight. Its wings flap,
And a lone feather twirls softly down
From the high rafters,
As it swoops out a broken window.

Small Man

This morning I visited De Leon.
A small man crumpled up in dirty sheets
On a torn mattress.
I sat at the end of his bed. He told me
Stories of the many men he had seen killed
In the streets. He asked me:
Have you ever seen one die?
I am going to change my life he said.
I saw his crutches in one corner.
When I left his room, walked down the stairs,
It was night already. The sky would not open,
Though it was lined with a voice,
And I with so many questions.

Cloudy Day

It is windy today. A wall of wind crashes against,
windows clunk against, iron frames
as wind swings past broken glass
and seethes, like a frightened cat
in empty spaces of the cellblock.

In the exercise yard
we sat huddled in our prison jackets,
on our haunches against the fence,
and the wind carried our words
over the fence,
while the vigilant guard on the tower
held his cap at the sudden gust.

I could see the main tower from where I sat,
and the wind in my face
gave me the feeling I could grasp
the tower like a cornstalk,
and snap it from its roots of rock.

The wind plays it like a flute,
this hollow shoot of rock.
The brim girded with barbwire
with a guard sitting there also,
listening intently to the sounds
as clouds cover the sun.

I thought of the day I was coming to prison,
in the back seat of a police car,
hands and ankles chained, the policeman pointed,
    "See that big water tank? The big
     silver one out there, sticking up?
     That's the prison."

And here I am, I cannot believe it.
Sometimes it is such a dream, a dream,
where I stand up in the face of the wind,
like now, it blows at my jacket,
and my eyelids flick a little bit,
while I stare disbelieving. . . .

The third day of spring,
and four years later, I can tell you,

how a man can endure, how a man
can become so cruel, how he can die
or become so cold. I can tell you this,
I have seen it every day, every day,
and still I am strong enough to love you,
love myself and feel good;
even as the earth shakes and trembles,
and I have not a thing to my name,
I feel as if I have everything, everything.

I Am with Those

                    Whose blood has spilled on streets too often,
surprising bypassers in hushed fear
and withdrawal, and later over supper
tell of the bad one and good cops,
the bad one in a dark cell, the cop
goggle eyed on laughter.

                    I don't want weak people. I don't want
people to believe I am bad,
without knowing me first,
without giving me a chance to show my hand,
these people, scattered over the world,
in fluffy silks and puffy wallets and pockets,
I'll say nothing to, because it is they
who must learn now from me, who must hear me out.

                    I've seen too much, felt such strong love
and hurt in me, for the downcast, the criminal, the worker.
I'm not in love with money, with people I am,
I'm not hanging onto lies to save my skin,
I'm not for the one down when he or she is wrong,
I am for peace, for giving a man a chance
to prove himself, giving a woman her fair due.

                    Big men, gun-toting sheriffs, Cadillac cruising
gents, slick skinned ladies, you do not intimidate me,
I do not hold you higher than the next man
convicted of murder, or the next woman
believed to be bad.

                    I am dangerous. I am a fool to you all.
Yes, but I stand as I am,
I am food for the future,
my thought will blossom tomorrow,
today, I plant roots, and god help me,
I will not sell out, in the face of death,
and that is saying something so large, so very large,
                                        it scares me.

                    But more than fear, is my love of justice,
                    more than my pride, is to step aside
                    when someone is right. But today, no one speaks
                    the truth, yesterday, no one spoke the truth,

                    none stood up to say I was right, because
I stood alone, without money, without connections,
so today I stand up, I speak up, and stand with others
who do the same.
                    This is suffering, pain, anguish, and loneliness,
but also strength, hope, faith, love, it gives a man
those secret properties of the Spirit, that make a man a man,
it gives to us, what is most lacking,
most powerful and full of extreme beauty and body.

It Started

To Richard and Rex

        A little state-funded barrack
in the desert, in a prison. A poetry workshop,
an epicenter of originality, companionship,
pain and openness,

                              For some,
the first time in their life writing,
for others the first time saying openly what they felt,
the first time finding something in themselves,
worthwhile, ugly and beautiful.

        I think of you and me. Last night I was
thinking of you. I am your friend. I don't want you
to think otherwise.

        I was thinking, when we first wrote to each other.
        I remember instances, of tremendous joy
        when receiving your letters,
        what cells I was in,
        what emotional state, under
        what circumstances.
        Your letters always fell like meteorites
        into my lap.
        You were my first friendship
        engendered in this state, perhaps,
        all my past life.

I showed you my first poem ever written,
        "They Only Came To See the Zoo"

        But you didn't treat me like a wild ape,
        or an elephant. You treated me like Jimmy.
        And who was Jimmy?
A mass of molten fury in this furnace of steel,
and yet, my thoughts became ladles, sifting carefully
through my life, the pain and endurance,
to the essence of my being,
        I gently, into the long night, unmolding
        my shielded heart, the fierce figures
        of war and loss, I remolding them,
        my despair and anger into a cry and song,
I took the path alone, nuded myself to my own caged animals,
and learned their tongues and their spirits,
and roamed the desert, went to my place of birth. . . .

Now tonight, I am a burning bush,
my bones a grill of fire,
I burn these words in praise,
of our meeting, our friendship.

To My Own Self

My hands the   Hook thunder hangs its hat on,
My breast the Arroyo storms fill with water,
My brow the   Horizon sunrise fills,
My heart the   Dawn weaving blue threads of day,
My soul the   Song of all life. . . .

Against

I saw the moon at first one blue twilight,
standing, blowing drops of breath into cold air,
standing in my prison jacket, 4:30,
in the compound, circled with high granite walls,
not a stir, but glare of spotlights, the silent
guard towers and stiff-coated guards above them all,

A big bloated desert moon, there,
how held up, such a big moon? Such a passionate tear!
How, against the velvety spaciousness of purple sky,
how does it hold itself up, and so close to me! To me!

Tell me! What should it mean,
that a moon like a wolf's yellow eye
should stare into my eye directly?
My finger, had I raised my arm,
could have punctured it like a peach and on my head
sweet juice drips, I could have pushed my finger in,
retrieved the seed of its soul, the stern hard pupil,
and placed it upon my tongue, sucked its mighty power

of dreams! Dreams, for how I needed them,
how I howled inside, sweeping great portions of thoughts
away with steel blue blades of the hour,
this, the time of my imprisonment.

I split days open with red axes of my heart,
the days falling like trees
I chopped up into each hour
and threw into the soul's fire.

I had not known the desert's power back then.
I had not known the black-footed demons
pecking each lightray as if it were straw.
I had not known my dreams, diamond hard,
could break at the silence of dragging winds;
no, nor that a pebble could come to mean
a world, unlocking fear. . . .

I looked into that moon, amazed, never
having seen a moon so much mine,
gathering my plundered life into its arms,

Moon! Moon! Moon! that twilight morning,
on the way to the kitchen to have some coffee,
thinking of my ten years to do in prison,
bundled up in my jacket, my boots feeling good and firm,
walking on under the guard's eye, blinded and blank-eyed,
to my escape, my freedom just then,
the guard's ears clogged, deaf,
when the moon said, "You are free,
as all that I have, winds, mountains, you are free. . . .

How We Carry Ourselves

To Others in Prisons

I am the broken reed in this deathly organ,
I am those mad glazed eyes staring from bars,
the silent stone look
that knows like other stones the smell of working feet,
knows how long and wide a human can spread
over centuries,
each step, until we now step on dust
and rock of prisons.

I could not throw my feelings away,
shoot them like wild horses,
stone them like weeping dirty prophets,
could not machete them pioneering a new path,
I sought no mountain, no brave deed,
I sought to remain human, to look and feel wind bless me. . . .

Chicanos, Blacks, Whites, Indians,
we are all here, our blood all red,
we are all filled with endurance
and have tasted the blade,
smelled the gun's oily smoke of death.

We are steel hunks of gears and frayed ropes,
our hands the toolsheds,
our heads the incessant groan
of never ending revolving wheels
in an empty, gaunt warehouse,
our blood dripping from steel joints
like grease and oil onto granite floors.

I meant to say, you can turn away from this:
if you can take the hammering, they will give,
if you can hold on while they grip you
and hurl you ragefully at the ground,
if you can bite your teeth when they bend you,
and still, you do not fit,
you can be who you are.

You can see the morning and breathe in God's grace,
you can laugh at sparrows, and find love
in yourself for the sun, you can learn
what is inside you, you can know silence,

you can look at the dark gray machine around you,
souls going up like billows of black smoke,
and decide what you will do next,
you who are the main switch, who turns
everything off.
But you breathing, smiling, struggling,
turning yourself on. . . . . .

There Are Black

There are black guards slamming cell gates
on black men,
And brown guards saying hello to brown men
with numbers on their backs,
And white guards laughing with white cons,
and red guards, few, say nothing
to red inmates as they walk by to chow and cells.

There you have it, the little antpile . . .
convicts marching in straight lines, guards flying
on badged wings, permits to sting, to glut themselves
at the cost of secluding themselves from their people . .
Turning off their minds like watertaps
wrapped in gunnysacks that insulate the pipes
carrying the pale weak water to their hearts.

It gets bad when you see these same guards
carrying buckets of blood out of cells,
see them puking at the smell, the people,
their own people slashing their wrists,
hanging themselves with belts from light outlets;
it gets bad to see them clean up the mess,
carry the blue cold body out under sheets,
and then retake their places in guard cages,
watching their people maul and mangle themselves,

And over this blood-rutted land,
the sun shines, the guards talk of horses and guns,
go to the store and buy new boots,
and the longer they work here the more powerful they become,
taking on the presence of some ancient mummy,
down in the dungeons of prison, a mummy
that will not listen, but has a strange power
in this dark world, to be so utterly disgusting in ignorance,
and yet so proudly command so many men. . . .

And the convicts themselves, at the mummy's
feet, blood-splattered leather, at this one's feet,
they become cobras sucking life out of their brothers,
they fight for rings and money and drugs,
in this pit of pain their teeth bare fangs,
to fight for what morsels they can. . . .

And the other convicts, guilty
of nothing but their born color, guilty of being innocent,
they slowly turn to dust in the nightly winds here,
flying in the wind back to their farms and cities.
From the gash in their hearts, sand flies up spraying
over houses and through trees,

        look at the sand blow over this deserted place,
you are looking at them.

On a September Day

I stand listening to a young man,
twenty-one, twenty-two, wondering why
he ever came to Arizona from Chicago.

Here's hell in red burning sky, but
I love it and can't stand a soft-skinned one
complaining about it, as he does.
Or bringing out lotions and fancy do-dads
jingling all over the body like a dork.
No wonder creatures crawl away into nooks.

Five years, five long years, behind these walls,
and still, I've yet to get an answer,
except from the quiet ones, who say everything
with their eyes.

I can see the Florence courthouse
from my cell window. And out at the field,
after running a few miles around,
I'll pause and look out there to Florence.

There's a chain gang pulling and hoeing weeds
by the prison preacher's house.
A big horse behind them, as
brown and black backs sweat and bend in sun. . . .

Preacher and courthouse standing above,
and below them black/brown bodies bend.
In my heart a jackhammer suddenly explodes
the hard rock I've placed over it. . . .
I almost want to cry, things are so fucked up. . . .

Why ain't they tearing the bricks out
of the courthouse that has never given them justice,
why don't they burn the preacher's house down,
that lazy glob of pulpish meat with blue
hard crystal eyes damning them from a shade tree
where he sips tea,
why doesn't that guard on the horse get down,
and tell them to quit working like slaves,
that it's all wrong, the whole mess is
out of hand! Tell them, goddammit!

But the anger and hurt and love
clears mistily before my eyes,
and I turn, sweating bronze brow, drenched body,
and run another lap, my first clenched up,
trying to run the ache out of my heart.

I Ask Myself, Should I Cry? Or Laugh?

I am like a glossy green leaf, sticking out
in midnight moon, waxy drum-skin the moon pounds with wind. . . .
Guilt itches my heart, as though a grasshopper,
chewing half, or a thick lazy caterpillar spinning silk nets,
hanging blue raindrops, baskets that carry invisible rocks,
that crack their stomachs, making wings of my eyelids.
Should I cry or laugh, thinking of you,
you?

An old woman on bent legs and burning green eyes,
what did you do on Saturday afternoons, in your small trailer?
Like a whitening sandbar, as the days took more and more
of your dark healthy grains, pressing against the current
of age, your tongue printed in sand washed over silently
by water, malevolent water, a ripple washing your
thunder-jeweled life, under, under, sweet pearl of mine.

Mother of my mother, after being moved away,
a small child clutching pennies you gave me from a purse
hidden and hooked with a pin, next to your breasts. . . .
You showed me a picture of my mother, said
she was a good woman, and pictures of my uncles, killed
in wars, their airplanes hut-hut-hut-hutting out,
hurtling down the blue gray sky in a crying fire.

I saw their pictures, all of them,
but when you showed the one of my mother, a white flare of love
exploded in me, cascading down my naked soul,
as though a waterfall, in which I bathed.

But you? Your trailer in a weedy lot,
crocheting tableclothes rich as butterfly wings, pillowcases
designed as sun spreading on dawn-colored silk,
thick-fingered frontiering heart in your wild loneliness,
bad-mouthing my father's drunkenness softly,

in your little trailer, with a toaster, cloth
potholder, tiny-windowed low-ceilinged box, a jewel case
to you, where your memories sang from each night. . . .
I wanted to stay with you forever! To find
the truth, to ask and ask and ask, an orphan boy! Swirling
with stallion storms in me!

49

I could not ride, set free into your wood-wind
throat, that sang me calm in your great box-canyon, dripping
water, and silence that shone in our eyes;
            our love, our confusion, our fears, tumbled
like massive boulders down our red-veined hearts,
thousand and thousand of years old,
covering the shards and death skulls of your life,
holding the ocean of my future, my prehistoric hunger
for gods and demons unleashed, satiated by you, weaver woman.
            You died while I was in prison,
            This poem is for you, my one.

Unity of Hearts

Fan blades, propellers beating,
thudding the engine of flesh red hot, sucking in hot air
in heaving tired mouths,
dust stuck to lips, that open like blood scabs,
at golden fingernails
clawing your faces, workers of the fields.

Not all the cotton you've picked in forty years,
could absorb the tears
you feel for your children,

not an apple or orange as fresh and lively,
as red as a child's heart
or as sweetly juiced with youth,

not a root so valuable and deep
digs as does their laughter;

not a sun so high and spread so far as your anger, workers,

nothing split more than your hearts,
nothing more rotten than the taste of low wages,
nothing older than the young who work in fields,

in your old shoes and hats and clothes, durable and desertlike,
cactus-spun lizard-fingered wing-souls,

your sighs like feathers dropping lightly,
your eyes the mustard-colored desert mounds,
patience, and patience, and patience,
where mirages pose for your thirsty hearts . . .
fan blades raising dust clouds down farm roads,
in rusty old trucks and cars.

I Am Offering This Poem

I am offering this poem to you,
since I have nothing else to give.
Keep it like a warm coat
when winter comes to cover you,
or like a pair of thick socks
the cold cannot bite through,

        I love you,

I have nothing else to give you,
so it is a pot full of yellow corn
to warm your belly in winter,
it is a scarf for your head, to wear
over your hair, to tie up around your face,

        I love you,

Keep it, treasure this as you would
if you were lost, needing direction,
in the wilderness life becomes when mature;
and in the corner of your drawer,
tucked away like a cabin or hogan
in dense trees, come knocking,
and I will answer, give you directions,
and let you warm yourself by this fire,
rest by this fire, and make you feel safe,

        I love you,

It's all I have to give,
and all anyone needs to live,
and to go on living inside,
when the world outside
no longer cares if you live or die;
remember,
        I love you.

Confused and Amazed Again

By this life we lead:

The rat-tat-tat of hammers,
and crops fat and willing as our own children
to give us nothing or everything.

I am amazed by life's bottom layer of people,
with our fingers in dirt
plying our very souls thick with rain and sun,
combed by winds, dressed up with seasons,
where we slowly fall in despair,
then blossom up and out like water pushing
and pushing, swirling in mud,
we heavy with things to do.

Covering the world with this layer, a moving organic
assembly of sweat and blood and muscles, moving prisms
that glitter in sunlight and dim in moonlight,
attracting the heart, as no other light,

two rays, one human and the other earthly,
shooting far out into space,
far out giving future its eyes,
surrounded with utter darkness,

two rays,
that blind the gods, burn their fingers,
use the light, like rocks to catch fire
and warm them, give them light in darkness,
to breathe out the next dawn.

Oppression

Is a question of strength,
of unshed tears,
of being trampled under,

and always, always,
remembering you are human.

Look deep to find the grains
of hope and strength,
and sing, my brothers and sisters,

and sing. The sun will share
your birthdays with you behind bars,
the new spring grass

like fiery spears will count your years,
as you start into the next year;
endure my brothers, endure my sisters.

It Goes by Many Names

And behind the eyeball it sucks it empty,
scrapes it dry of sight like a kitchen pan, scoured silver
and hard. But not like before, when the heart would pick up
its drumsticks and pound the eyes like drums, or scoop
up water from rivers in healthy perceptions, not these eyes.
They dangle in skulls like little iron bells
set for ritual, some bewitching ceremony:
Blood in glass tubes rising; teeth clenching
and that rag knotted round the arm, bloating blood vessels,
to a plump swell of purple, pierced by a shiny needle, and
the heroin slides in, mixes with heart's life, across its
cheek like a sudden unfelt gash, opening to emptiness, to
a dizzy shower of darkness, smoothing across mind, a flooding
lake with barest ripples ribbing themselves through muscles,
ironing them out to sagging tired meat, in the warm heat
of heroin.
This is the new king.

His whip so gentle on bones of my people. His voice luring,
seductive in its slow torture. It is our flesh that covers
Him with warmth, and our legs that carry him over mountains.
His black seed in the womb of our blood,
like a black sun whose sunrays are our very blood, and
splintered lives, spreading out over everything, into the hurting
eyes of our loved ones, its dark glow, glowing.
So few can rebel against his mothering chains, suckling
grains from his breasts, and pain from his fingertips.
When he leaves, the land is cold, and when present,
how very warm and beautiful. Each bough ablack, blossom blacker,
until nothing is seen, nothing, there is nothing, the last
flicker fading, into the king's cup, who drinks up lives,
and lives, and lives.
And all the drug centers, the counselors,
the prison sentences, the ravages upon society, upon families,
upon the future, all of these are like dry leaves under
its golden boot, like sweet meat to its burly hungers,
like sails under its wind, blowing us all farther into its dark sea.
All my people are behind bars for taking heroin.
But they are not criminals. They are under its spell, as others
are under the spell of money, ambition, lucrative living,
and others want to learn secrets of wisdom, as those under
the horrors of jealousy: *they* are not criminals; or are they?

Nixon points his finger, the atom bomb points,
the tearing up of earth points, the dirtying of our waters points,
and so I point, not to my people, they are not criminals, I point
to our ignorance, our shambled souls, our greed and easy living,
our dull minds.

Cry and scream to me, You are wrong! Wrong! Wrong!
And I will listen to you, and look long upon your face, and
weep for you, be silent for you, assist you. And together,
none of us being wrong, I will take your hand, and we will
find our solutions, and the great king will be no more, or
will hobble on crutches and beg for crumbs at each gate,
of our wise culture, and be turned away, to hide in the hills
where now we imprison our brothers and sisters.

Selected Early Poems

Healing Earthquakes

Through little garden plots I was mesmerized by,
Through streets torn and twisted like gnawed bark,
Through all the writers and artists of Americas
Parading by my fathers, I with their quills and
                                                brushes,
Through all the stately documents,
Those of the Bible and political bodies of the
                                                world,
And quietly by itself is the Healing Earthquake,
From all sides it comes,
Through the black-knotted drunkenness of my
                                                father,
Through the cold deep bowels of hope,
Through the trowels of sombrero'd brick-layers
And wall-builders spreading the moist mortar,
Through the blacks in the South in grimy torn
                                                t-shirts,
To the snarling CIA that broke loose from their
                                                chains,
To the crumbled houses of my people,
Through the scorpion-tailed magnums and
                                                carbines
Held at their heads,
Healing Earthquake comes up from the debris
                                                and rubble,
Splitting its own body and heart,
Mumbling below in its own discontented winds,
Threading slowly my torn soul in a grip of fury,
To the eye of its mark it leans undaunted,
I am Healing Earthquake,
Not in the commotion swirling upwards of the atom
                                                bomb,
Nor the blast and heraldic upshoot of a rocket,
A lesser man by all the law books,
A man awaking to the day with ground to stand upon
                                                and defend.

By Invitation of My Soul

I have been struggling to do as I could in my
      Ignorance against the wise wickedness of this
Around me, and it is so beautiful to know I
      Have not relinquished that bond with my soul.
I have not won the battle, but I am in a
      Condition where I will grow stronger with the
Passing Days, and the enemy will tire himself
      Out, a nation of enemies, a nation of untruth,
In the face of a truth, a faith, a belief,
      Can withstand them, indeed overcome them.
Yet it frightens me to this day
      That a man can become so weak as I.
Is it my weakness or the great evil strength of them?
      I am led to believe it was my weakness.
The fragileness of an undirected lamb
      That survives among blood-tooth'd wolves.
I have had to harden my carcass, my nice
      Soft fleece knots and falls away, my gums
Decay, my hoofs crack, my eyes pour molten
      Globs of tears in the blizzards of these days,
Yet those who look upon the mountain
      From their green valley, shall see this lamb
Balance itself on the sharp edge of the
      Highest rock, where if he falls, the falls are
Of the longest and cruelest, though only
      In such heights when all is destroyed, does
The soul extend its wings and balance on
      Winds, on Winds of freedom, of true heaven,
Of freedom. There is the lamb who lives in
      The rocks, among the rocks, who has nothing
To offer but his silence, for it is here in the
      Silence where he contemplates his wrongs,
His beauty, God recognizes as his prayers.
      So what are walls of prison?
They have come from the earth, and now
      Weep silently wishing to return to their home.
They are like me, they are in prison,
      They are my teachers, I learn from them.
They are symbols of the world, mankind's

Vertebrate that yellows with bird droppings
    And rain.
It is a curtain of a play with no words,
    A play
That says the sun is a period of one sentence,
    In its quest to conquer.
A play that joins its pages with gold lace
    With words written in the blood of the
Defeated, the wall is a wafer of morphine
    To the painfully fearful, it is a mosquito
That bites the whole town falling into a
    Deep fever for more blood and more blood
And more blood, a mosquito I crush
    Between my thumb and forefinger
And crush well, like a mother,
    And feed it to my pet cockroaches in my cell.

The Body

Feeling the bars,
Running my fingers over them,
Smearing with blood, bugs,
And bits of dried food.
                    A forest of bars . . .
The flesh must toughen to the cold,
Must callous to the rock,
I must learn to heal my own wounds,
Clack the rocks of my heart together
To bring fire,
And bleed the poisons from my body
In the fields where I sweat,
Walking quiet not to disturb
The great apes and tigers,
Walking carefully around traps
With sharp little bamboo shanks,
Camouflaged in socks and cloth shirts
Of the hunters and the hunted.

*   *   *

santiago baca to inman, 5 may 1977. . . . there are
mountainous regions we have yet to map out within
our voices, the themes . . . are sometimes great signs
pointing the way . . . they are not domesticated—
they are tribal songs to be shared by all . . . no one
can keep them for themselves. because humanity
spins through them, not individually but as a
whole nation/tribe lofted up or ground down to
fine powder in the wind, water, fire and earth,
the poems are signs that tell us things. if we
place them side by side, we see they point to a
direction. they have broken from the circle of
today's petrification in the cities and have left a
gaping hole in the fence. if they patch the hole
up so none of the slaves will get ideas about free-
dom, trust that i will be behind there to barrel
thru again. and i am not afraid of the hunting
parties and passels of critics that will tag at my
heels. we can lose them easy enough. but they
will be blind in our world. . . .

A Song of Survival

I worked as a licensed plumber, had my own tools
and truck, every morning met the sun, felt my muscles
pull against each other, working the pipe-wrenches
and shovels. I worked as a business executive for a
merchandise firm, meeting customers, having coffee
in cafes with prospective clients, feeling the sturdy
handshakes, wearing my new white shirts and suits of
different colors, driving automatic, power-steering
chevvies, travelling to small communities,
and I worked in Mexico as a rock-breaker, high on
the mountain, stood in the midday sunlight,
shirtless, my chest shimmering in perspiration, as I
brought the big hammer down on huge rocks,
cracking them,
and my chest heaving, my legs apart, both hands
gripped tight, and down again on the rock!
And I worked for myself as a dope dealer of
marijuana, sitting with friends on lawns,
in living rooms,
or by the sea, we'd sit and watch the sun going down,
glistening over a thousand tiny swelling curls of water,
exploding orange and yellow on the horizon,
and I wondered about my life, where I
wanted it to go, deciding what I wanted from life.
And I worked as a woodchopper in the mountains,
the snow was marvelous,
glittering in the morning with the smell of wood
everywhere, fresh wet bark, speckled with dew,
and broken sticks oozing sap, tree boughs
shaking with squirrels, deer on their pointing toes
watched me from a distance eyes brimming with sparks.
And I worked as a dishwasher,
two big stainless steel sinks filled with tumultuous
heaps of pans and skillets and chef-spoons,
big-bellied pots with burned black bottoms, with
sleeves rolled up and rubber apron on, I'd bend over,
scrubbing as fast as I could, while waitresses
zing'd back and forth, dumping pans and dishes,
giving me a word of consolation—I'd grump,

and they'd scurry away tired as myself.
I worked as a streetsweeper in the early morning
in my heavy old jacket and cap, pushing the broom,
picking up papers, musing over the display windows
of department stores, admiring women embarking
on the bus, their thighs pressed smoothly against
skirts, hair flowing, eyes jet dark and soft lips,
while their hair shook, and winds sped rowdily
down streets, against curtains of windows, against
shiny hair of businessmen, their shoes spit polished
to a gleam, briefcase in hand, and, soon, all the
people jumbling across stoplights, cars and trucks
sputtering in the early morning.
And I worked as a cook and bouncer in a niteclub,
cooking hamburgers and fish,
carrying out drunks and breaking up fights,
shooting pool with my friends as they choked
on the food, and the drunks staggered back in,
pushing cars late at night to get them started.
And I worked as a milker in a big dairy farm,
loving the cows,
I'd walk down the old path to the fields with a stick
in my hand, they'd all turn with groggy brown eyes,
slowly swishing tails and chewing cuds,
I'd give a whistle, they'd come to me, I'd follow
them down the path, talking to them as they
mosey'd on, and I'd tell them I loved them, their
big wet noses.
And I worked as a truckdriver in town at night,
in the small cab, with just me, the radio, the stars,
and the empty streets,
and I'd stop by a residential house with a big garden
and snip a few roses in the dark,
then jump back in my truck and drive down to my
woman's house, tap on the glass pane, I'd hear
her mother's worried voice ask who would come to
the window, and my woman would open the curtain,
smile sleepily, and run to the door to let me in.
And I worked as a metalworker on top of bridges,
tying strips of metal bars together before they
poured the cement, and at noon I'd have armwrestles
with the carpenters,
and eat chili, sitting on dirt mounds, my whole body
aching from work, yet I was proud, and I'd drive

the big scrapers, and direct the man in the crane,
and help carpenters, they'd invite me over
to their trailers in the evening,
and, finally, when the bridge was done, we all
stood there, looking proud in our dirty and
dust-smudged faces, and knew the bridge
meant something to us all.
I owned a chuckwagon filled with icy cokes and
candy bars and hot sandwiches, I would go around
to all the construction sites, and beep beep the gas
horn, and out of the massive and rambling
construction site, grubby workmen began appearing,
out of windows, out of brick heaps and holes in the
ground, plumbers, electricians, carpenters,
laborers, all lining up,
their tools and instruments jangling and knocking
from heavy leather belts at their waists, the sun
beating down fiercely. I'd give them cokes and
candy, and we'd joke, while they squatted down
and ate, smoked a cigarette, brushed dust from
their faces and hair, talked about the buildings,
blueprints, materials.
And I worked as a school custodian, pushing the
long dust-mop down the shiny scuffed halls,
passing the numbered doors, cleaning desks,
windows, scrubbing toilets and walls, watering
the grass and watching the kids play basketball,
I, the only person among all these books,
blackboards and little figures of cut paper
thumbtacked to boards, little gold and blue stars,
and colored drawings on paper, as I
swept up the dirt and carried my dustpan out,
emptying trashcans—
not only school, but the whole world, would be
empty, empty without children, the most
precious creatures of God, our hopes and loves.
And I went on working at different jobs,
as a chain-puller, a soda-jerk, a shoe salesman,
refrigeration mechanic, gardener, horse trainer,
appliance man, painter—I searched
for an occupation where I could expend my full
worth, I needed a job
where I could be free and creative, and I kept
searching, learning about people, about the

country, while I looked for something to define my
heart with the world into one, using my body and
mind and soul, into one,
and the search led me to my first cell in prison.

I thought to myself, here is the ultimate test of
survival, I have lost all I've known, and now,
between these four walls, where a man can
touch ceiling with his hand and extend both arms
and touch both walls, here, then
is the test of my heart, my soul, all that I am.
And I died a little bit, my past life dissolved,
drew into an empty pit in my heart,
like rain water in potholes, and the world's
wheels splashed through it every minute,
going somewhere, and leaving me,
as if a hitchhiker on a distant road in the middle
of nowhere, at night, alone, and all the faces
I had known melted in the dark night,
the sunsets and sunrises bleared pale, gone,
all the voices, the laughter, words of workmen,
their smells, the motion of their muscles, their
deep understanding eyes, mornings, all gone,
distilled in the horrible words of a judge
and my sentence, all gone to just my face,
to hands no longer feeling tools, or dirt and bread
in toolboxes, to legs that no longer climb
or walk long distances . . . no longer, but
shortened to a five by nine cell, my whole life
stuffed into this cell,
no more working with machines or touching roots
or petals, no more hearing the mad sputter of engines,
no more seeing a woman's eyes,
no more children's voices or their running back and
forth, no more freeways packed with cars with
thousands of faces freshly scrubbed and hair combed,
no more arms holding other arms
or people playing with each other in the parks,
no more ladies in shorts with beautiful legs,
or tall men and short men laughing genuinely,
all wearing different clothes, bouncing on their toes,
and the soft voices of their breast, or the roaring,
no more, just silence
in the middle of the night, as I
look past the grilled bars, out over the bobwire,

and between the gun towers, I don't feel dead,
yet I know something has died in me,
something dies this moment,
and I asked in a whisper, What will you do now?

I must connect life with my heart, I must bring it
to me! I must reach across the walls with my soul
and call loud out to life, out to people I love,
out to life I dearly love—they cannot keep it
from me!

I hear in my heart lovers singing of life and love
and sorrow, and there is still the voice within me,
none can drown or take it away,
and I follow the voice to its destination,
along the way I pass my own death, my own dying,
my voice roars inside for freedom! for love! for work!
For survival, for a chance to be myself, to overcome,
and to live! to live! to live myself!
I looked long at the walls, at the bars, at the bobwire,
I looked long out over them to the distance
and beyond, to the horizon,
and knew I would die here, and must struggle like a
child, to reknow myself, to relearn my heart,
to live after I have died, to bring myself up from my
knees, like a man who has never walked before,
who is crippled in the face of great adversity,
I must rise on hope alone, a small unknown man,
a young man that loves songs and people's kindness,
though what I had been they took away, all of it,
each particle, all torn from me and destroyed, away,
gone, and I am left with myself, my heart, my soul,
my mind—in complete shock, in utter frenzy of
visions, in incalculable depths of desire,
my whole person busted up, kicked and broken,
folded up in a cloth of fire, its ashes floating out
into oblivion, there was nothing. . . .

There was nothing, but to eat, sleep and live in this
cell, a boisterous clamor of despair in my soul,
shields and swords of new thoughts and new feelings,
all unanswered, bursting and chanting
the unfulfilled desires, all devastating this man.
My cell was square, squareness effused from each
corner, each particle of the cell's existence,
the plain bed of gray steel,

the green walls, the steel cabinet, it was a cradle
and a grave, to begin anew,
to die so young, unmourned, uncelebrated except by
me.
All my life had been led among old and young trees,
rocks, dirt roads and evening walks.
Now between these four walls,
Life, you must come from me, the shoes you admired
in stores, the unfulfilled plans you carefully
charted, the lovely ones you sought to kiss and love,
must come from within you.
My soul stung, became murky and heavy like wax,
the grasslands within me rotted, the fullness
disgorged, became gaunt as a web of stairwells,
climbing, single soul, lovely and mournful one,
haggard and blind, you climb O soul of mine!
Yes, it was here in this cell, in the dry air,
the bleached bone walls offering loneliness,
the wretched sinews of my heart
uncoiled despair from each grain of breath and
blood, you straggled gray-whiskered soul of mine!
A stallion and child at times,
a tree, a rock, a sound, a house you become,
in your own company, celebrating your own
understood celebrations, festive and conceited
for a leaf falling your way,
Here within these walls, you become the world,
mother to your flesh, father to your son,
son to your father, all in one, you become!
And traveled beyond the limits of thirst,
suffered beyond the limits of anguish,
a rampage of questions in your wake,
heedless Challenger, Escorter of the void!
Haltered by a secret wisdom of the seasons,
plying at the sun, drilling deep within me,
you sink, you sink, you sink, explorer beyond time!

Losing touch with civilization, with what is right
and wrong, with roads of ambition, with the term
love, as you turned through the damp caves of your
being, to find ungreen craters of your identity,
to find your eyes like rocks among papers and
books of bygone days, weeping with joy,
shuddering claps of thunder in my veins,
you stepped through each divine cavern,

their blood-red roofs, their blue walls and wooden
floors, air, water, dogs, supper, these elements
drove like Springs across your eyes, grew from your
touch, your desire, like late blossoms, fields
rich and aplenty for the world you were,
are, shall always be.

Soul of mine, small or great is of your choice,
but among the trees you came small, a child,
among rocks and people's laughter, the cooking
of eggs, trucks and jeans, alfalfa fields
in their blanket of greenish mist and musk,
you came small and humble,
sweeping across me, Gatherer of Sunlight,
yourself, a massive heft of field in me!

But among this clandestine house, bereft of human
noise, that consigns life to a planet,
on this alien and petrified phantom, a semblance
of land and life so bleak, bleak to its core,
each slice of life's juicy meat
tossed out, dry and infertile as cattle carcass
gnawed by wolves on some destitute plain,
here in this wilderness of injustice,
where law is raw and savage, a ray of anguish
through lonely hearts, multiplied is the hurt
like gasping waves in a storm,
that touches the unmoving rock of my wisdom,
fitted to its own inclinations, its own reign under
the thorned crown, elected by fate, unwilling
to give up this pauper audience,
I, my spirit become aboriginal of the spirit world,
kneeling on blood-blotched sand
along the inner rims of my skull, blistered hot as
a furnace, to sip the lakes of light
as I traveled into oblivion, on a hunt for more
oblivion, in the hope I would scale the secrets it
held, secure them between my teeth,
to withstand the pain of my loneliness, the
amputation of worlds for other worlds,
this world where I found my legs and arms were
unloved, my limbs mere labor digits
for my prosecutors.
My heart and head pounded fiercely,
neglected, confirmed as unfit, where each single

pore and slab of muscle, each hair,
my lips, my lashes, my fingers, toes, step—
all became useless, unadmired, confined,
ridiculed by these monsters of an unmerciful justice,
all I was, erased in this rote-factory of human
beings, to bare bristling marches on cold black
mornings across the compound, to slave labor,
to numbers, to dispensing with my name, a land
without feeling, the eyes turned inward
to a foiled black rose, and, outward, just the barb
of its stem, through the pupil of each eye, arc'd,
the splattering bits of fire as the welders within
worked to close each crack of the cold soul.
I, my soul, became a salt flat, white and barren,
as my thoughts foamed saliva from their thirsty
mouths, I became conquistador of all evil a man
might want, I became death bereaving itself,
all I had known, gone, glowing like a pile of
coals, so glowing, my soul shaded itself from the
heat, but my loss glowed like the evening sun,
covering earth, leaving only my breathing
and dark night ahead.

Then came morning, daybreak, dawn, and
fresh it was, and I like a hunter
in a new forest filled with fowls and animals,
stepped gently into my loveliest hour,
it came for me, from me to me, a world,
a life time, many life times, compressed into one
hour of enlightenment,
an insight of love fully supped by me, fashioned
by me, to purge imprisonment;
and so much more I hadn't asked for, I received.
What does it mean, this passage of time,
blighted with furious contradictions, a flurry of
flung dreams and expectant miracles, arguments
on the stature and breadth of human beings,
the droning intoning of something within ourselves,
the persistent discharge of violence, raw
like birth spreading over the continents, what
does it mean?
Are we competent warriors rampaging in masks of
civilization?
Raw justice is sweeter and closer to our souls
than formal justice,

when our feet take us, toll the bells of life,
gentle tug of times past leap from earth,
hallucinations of our ancestry call to us,
from each point and form.

The mortar of these callous walls, what fingers
mixed it? From where was sand taken? From
places where Indians made their fires,
holy fires, where buffalos clouded the land,
where trappers and pioneer families stepped,
where newly freed slaves tramped, where holy
dancers hummed on heated dust, and seeds
were sown to bloom fresh fruit
offered to passing beggars and Spanish kings,
from this dust came life,
came imprisonment and oppression, also . . .

Someone knelt here a million years ago and let
the sand sift through real fingers, and
with thousands of years, came someone
who thought of building a home, a town, perhaps
a city, the best city in the world,
and there was water, so precious and little,
dampening dry lips of children, men and women,
animals and fowls of all kinds,
water that offered gold nuggets,
water bemused by flowery mountains,
water cutting rock supervised by winds,
water obeying the root's demands, water offering
its share of life to us humans, our share of life.

And faraway, or nearby, a million sparks
generated by the clash of swords—subsided
in the abundance of land, wheat and beans,
cucumbers and apples, and came
arid steel plows sweeping the rugged land
to a smooth, polished and baffling prosperity.
Our hands were heavy with goods and fruits—
the inventions of the land contracted the earth
to wood and water and land no longer pompous
or regal, land no more of illusions, no more
prayers, no more dances,
but each hand striking an element
till earth spastically shrivelled,
and clothed the culture of the new man.

71

Steel, sand, water, wood, how it all bears such
fortune for us, how it all blossoms into cities
and new miracles, how—I ask the steel, wood,
water, sand—how is it you do not crumble in my
hands when used for such evil purposes?
I sit and wonder over your obstinate virtue,
the wonder of your abilities to assist mankind,
and yet, pasteurized by politics and ambitious
bureaucrats, and yet they never patronized you
as did sons and daughters of this land, now ages
past—we submit to you our hearts and souls and
blood again! but this time to be free of you—
you have not changed, man has changed you
and led us all to believe you are something you
are not: to me, O Great Wall, you remain
the sand my grandfather's grandfather touched
to determine the passage of the hunt, where
deer and bison hoof'd, where moccasins and
sandals flashed beads around
fires in gold moonlight,
where sunlight gleamed on sweating brows and
burned rocks, O Great Wall, you have held
the bones of my people! came winter, you
clothed them in snow, came autumn
you whistled on harps of wind and collected
leaves; came spring, to those who survived you
and your ways, you gave fruit and nuts,
filled their shovels and loosened up their picks,
sturdy for the trundling loads of goods,
for the goats.
You were sanctuary for the meditator,
a vase for trees and crops, as sunlight licked your
canyons like kettles of brewing lakes and melting
snows, flying eagles.
You, O Great Wall, are not my enemy!
Here the men scrawl their last hopes on you,
as did their fathers' fathers' fathers,
journeying into unknown territory, as do their
sons who come to prison, yearlings lost
on barren rock, motherless, friendless men,
whose enemies do not inhabit the rock
but men's rocky hearts, as time
and more time and more time
floods the steel entrails of this beast,

as injustice flooded the land back then,
and, like then, we somehow survive, we
somehow survive.

You are as you are, O Great Wall,
hugging steel with your dry shoulders,
kissing the keys of jailers, placing your
immovable shoes of granite in my path,
crossing my eyes with your steel mesh wire.
I hibernate here like the invisible water of your
composition, remembering the many ditches I
swam on dry afternoons, the gladness and
easiness of my arms as they moved
to people—someday, when you fall and become
dust again, the people that run their fingers through
that dust, shall know my poem in their hearts
and smile, as I did when I was free to dig
and plant and walk, as I do now, in the heart
and soul of mine.
I work you, Great Wall, Great Great Wall!
I work your parched and bitter face,
your cracked and hard skull,
your steely endurance I work with my pen
in hand and heart, like a sledge hammer
pounding away, pounding! pounding!
with each desire of mine, a silver toothed sickle
swathing away the black brush of despair,
with my dreams clamping into you,
scratching out a beginning for me, as did my
father who came upon you sleeping,
unwilling to sprout crops for them until they
gave enough sweat, gave enough blood
defending you, though sons upon sons blistered
their young hands, though you cracked beneath
their shabby soles, as they dug deeper and deeper
into you, against your will, finally to bring
enough food to live, enough to let them live,
with honor, as men and women, so it is with me,
Great Wall. I have entered the cycle of life
again, they built you up with toil and sweat,
I break you down with my words,
disintegrate you into the wilderness you are,
for when I pace my cell, I pace on dust,
when I feel you with my hand, I feel the strum of
water, I see gold nuggets and flowers, scratches

of those who passed through here.
For my fathers to live according to the law of
the land, they had to build you, enclose
their folds of sheep and mark new black boundaries,
and for me to live, I must crumble the walls,
free if not any but myself from the fold
of prisoners, reclaim my manhood, this is the only
way, it is the circle of life, as cities fall
and are built again by other hands, reworking
what was wrong, so this is wrong and must fall.
And from dust blessed by many hands, I retrieve
their ancient dreams of a good life,
a good future and healthy children, I make my
tools—the written word against granite,
to bloom the muse each morning, that
lets me live, learn, and go on struggling,
that is all I ask and all I expect of myself,
for I am the wall of justice and refuse to crumble,
I am the wall of love and can shelter you,
I am with my woman who brings the next
generations that shall dance to stars and roots
yet to come, I am the wall that touches into deep
heavens, forth to all sides of the earth,
condensed it falls like water off my tongue, when I
speak, when I move boulders from the path I
wish to take.

I Am Who I Am

You ask me what has happened to the woman I love,
If I still love her. . . . I smile a lot to that question,
    A good and soft smile. I wonder myself about that question,
And that is why I smile. What has happened to her?
    She is slowly grafting herself into a woman.
I have fond memories of her. For the rest, all I know,
    is that I will live alone in this life,
though I constantly try to convince myself otherwise.
    Loneliness follows me through crowds like my own shadow
crossing over faces and bodies of the multitudes in the sun.
    Into the distance in myself I walk away, over the sanddunes
and through the mirages I walk into the distance and die.
    There are many worlds in me; though virile and young,
I cannot conquer them. Gripped by the teeth,
    by the words of a shaman, at the same time a romantic poet,
at the same time a priest and lover of the body,
    at the same time a farmer, I speak through all of them,
        a village developed by them all in one-ness I am,
so my home is their home, my food is their food.

But I was offered this or that, life or death,
and a third alternative: in a vision I was offered understanding
    of the spiritual world. I, however, in my ignorance, and
love of life, chose to experience the movement of a little finger,
    experience what people experience, from the tiny movement
of their lips, to their sighing death breath, with all my
    human frailty and futility, in my ignorance, I chose
that it will be by my hand that my life is carved and fragmented.

Love me in a way that is suited to you. If you must build walls
then build them. You are free to do as you wish.
    All people in life are. I will not supplicate others not to do
what they are doing. Each wall is different
    and each person is different, but they are never so high
that the sunshine will not enter inside. Try like hell,
    and still the sunshine will enter them.

Human beings are fantastic pavilions, tents you see in the night;
the glow of youth, beauty or money illuminates their faces,
    but still inside, we see a shadow pass behind the canvas eye,

still inside is where the test begins, to understand one's self,
   a very old man and very young child, constant and changing,
despising the same things that are loved,
   in its fervid beautiful crazy confusion,
dazed in its romance of the world, tragic in its ridiculous sadness,
   giving miracles to friends because it cannot give itself away,
living with loneliness that gives it all it needs,
   setting a plate of vegetables before the child,
asking the old man to wrestle mountains,
   in this way finding out who we are.

Through the Streets

Friday night whistles at young ladies, and holds others close to its fat heart, where Barry White sings on a wooden stool, in the cool smoke of feelings.

The Friday fields free themselves of week-long work, and white flowers fly from their hands, and lovers lie across the dips and grooves of grass.

Through the town, Friday rides. With lights on and music extra fired from horns and strings, the streets sink to a welcome passage, and fit the crowds and gaudy glare of grime and gold.

People plunge into the wave of late-night fun, and run their hearts on oily streaks, and dance on a dime or spin to the tune of a blues, and chuck the rhymes of weekly ringing bells and raging presidents, duck the world like a bishop in his mirroring clothing, and in robes and per-fumes and pleasant hails, huddle with crowds to crown the night with light.

The blinding light of town does not bother you, for it's the night that Jumbo Balloons sail over stadiums, and worked-on cars tear their tires on streets to the sweet giggle of growing bosoms.

Yes, the Wizard waves his wand, and un-afraid, the soft appearance of people forms around us. It is the night, when homes are sold for a drink, a woman for a shot of heroin and a pack of smokes, a thousand and thou-sand more, sexy the night, and the young lover carries a thousand hearts, and the old a thousand and thousand more.

Each State, each town, each small home, drinks up, decks out, and cards themselves to the stars, that sit around in glowing robes, and explode in frustrated fire, and curse across the night sky, unable to answer why, in droves, we undream the hours, and take our blood in hand, and let it sing, and cry, and laugh and scream.

For tomorrow we dream, and the stars will be sane again.

But tonight, tonight is Friday. It is to the people, like fish to the hungry horded before the lord's feet. It is the miracle that walks the bloody week in pure love, it is the rest one gets from its breath, invigorating our weak frames to the stature of Gods, followers of gods, whose kingdom is within them, vulnerable, shatterable, conquerable.

In the sky the moon is a dragon guarding the galaxy. And we below in dark bars, ooze to the blues, make magic of men, wine of women, and throw our hair into night's hand, that dyes it gray or young young black, in the morning when we wake.

Saturday, we feel like warriors, women and men, gently walking the grounds in light clothing. Our horses feed in the fields. And already we are thinking of the war come Monday.

The Day Brushes Its Curtains Aside

to a dark stage.

I lie there awake in my prison bunk,
in the eye-catching silence
of prison night.

I study the moon out my grilled window.
I figure this and that,
not out, just figure, figuring more,
the inner I go, through illimitable tunnels,

roaring great, myself back   back   back.

I lie still, listening to water drops
clink and pap   pap   pap
in the shower stall next to my cell.

In that airy place we call the heart,
I move like a magician
in colorful stage lights of my moods,
my bright dreams, and blue light
circles a tear on my cheek,
and lips with her name.

From flowers in my hands
her face appears. In cards
she is the queen. These are tricks
and I am the magician.

Tomorrow morning I will crawl out of bed,
knowing I cannot escape the chains
they've wrapped around me.

I will crawl out of bed tomorrow,
as though I had stepped out of a box
on stage. It was no illusion,
when the sword plunged into the box,
I smiled at the crowd,
as it went deeper and deeper into my heart.

A Desire

Out of the barbwire, the walls, the timeless days,
a desire forms in me, alongside my heart like a rock:
I stood with both feet squared and firm on the ground,
a ground made of rock, and I pounded that rock, until,
from the blast of my Will Power, a sliver of rock
sank into my heart, going deeper and deeper and deeper,
and no matter how I move, still, I cannot evade the pain of my
    weakness.

A desire is in me, as strong as any rock, as sharp as any:
it was the wall's hard hands, the barbwire's sharp nerve,
and Time's cruel endurance, all working in hand,
the pumice of a death, refining it, molding it,
and when I slept, it rose furiously from within me,
my flesh the hilt of its blade
that went down in me, so far, this silver root
of a new beginning; my tongue a steaming hot petal
in the cold new morning.

A desire heavy with furious flames throwing its dark shadow
on the lightness of life,
and all life seemed a glass window, and a flame there,
breathing against the thick glass,
churning its painful flames against the glass,
against flames against each other,
churning out shadows in creamy waves,
the cold wind avoiding the flames, beneath my eyes,
beneath my eyes were the flames and I filled with shadow.

The desire, the flame, pulled at the night;
the sleepy-skinned, soft and warm space of night
it drew into its sprawling glow of fingers.
And the night falling into its fiery palm,
untangling from contours of stars and moon,
ripped from the sky filling the fire
with a fragrance of it being all there was, all powerful—
my destiny, my only care. This pulsing desire
for new life, new ways of thinking, of seeing my humans,
unleashed a love-freedom in me, a freedom so free,
it took apart all I was, and put me together,
into all that I was not.

Rude

Life is so rude to me. Leaves my head
spinning like a hurled lid of a grease can,
wwwwoooorrrrringgg to a stop on cement;
creaked-up wood my bones, as it drives its green vines in me,
carves another year on me,
        battered by life like a rug at its front door:
        its heavy foot too quick, slides,
        and life lands on me, breaking a leg.
        I am shook out, hung on a line of tree boughs,
        and there ants and butterflies crawl over me,
        spiders usurp my knots and twines
        with silken nest for dew and eggs.

All this, living among drug addicts and blood,
among bottles of whiskey splintered in streets,
trashcans upended by black children playing warriors;
        Life is rude, rude as a knifeblade.
Life is a cord dangling with a death charge
while it sprays out light and sparks,
        this cord plugged into us, taped up with drugs
        and money wrapped around it,
        clamped by laws, silver shining laws;
        we are all electricians,
        looking for the short in the line,
        tearing out our walls and insulation.

        I have often seen that certain glow
        in a man's eye,
        and rings of energy flow from a woman's hand
        into mine, often that glow
        is what we call endurance and love,
        is why we do what we can't understand;
that glow is the sea where our treasures come to rest,
spilling out the gold coins and gems,
as the green tongues of our dreams shoot out
like a frog's in the grass bottom of sea,
swallowing the wingless treasures buried in sand of the past.

        Life is rude, is that rude guest we hope
        will never appear in our homes,

knocking like a stranger for a piece of bread,
stranger blown in by winds and snow,
traveling across America on an empty belly,
the one you hope will never come to your door,
looking in your eyes, without a word
telling you the truth of what you long tried to hide.

I Applied for the Board

. . . a flight of fancy and breath of fresh air
Is worth all the declines in the world.
It was funny though when I strode into the Board
And presented myself before the Council
With my shaggy-haired satchel, awiry
With ends of shoestrings and guitar strings
Holding it together, brimming with poems.

I was ready for my first grand, eloquent,
Booming reading of a few of my poems—
When the soft, surprised eyes
Of the chairman looked at me and said no.

And his two colleagues sitting on each side of him,
Peered at me through bluemetal eyes like rifle scopes,
And I like a deer in the forest heard the fresh,
Crisp twig break under my cautious feet,
As they surrounded me with quiet questions,
Closing in with grim sour looks, until I heard
The final shot burst from their mouths
That I had not made it, and felt the warm blood
Gush forth in my breast, partly from the wound,
And partly from the joy that it was over.

Who Understands Me But Me

They turn the water off, so I live without water,
they build walls higher, so I live without treetops,
they paint the windows black, so I live without sunshine,
they lock my cage, so I live without going anywhere,
they take each last tear I have, I live without tears,
they take my heart and rip it open, I live without heart,
they take my life and crush it, so I live without a future,
they say I am beastly and fiendish, so I have no friends,
they stop up each hope, so I have no passage out of hell,
they give me pain, so I live with pain,
they give me hate, so I live with my hate,
they have changed me, and I am not the same man,
they give me no shower, so I live with my smell,
they separate me from my brothers, so I live without brothers,
who understands me when I say this is beautiful?
who understands me when I say I have found other freedoms?

I cannot fly or make something appear in my hand,
I cannot make the heavens open or the earth tremble,
I can live with myself, and I am amazed at myself, my love,
my beauty,
I am taken by my failures, astounded by my fears,
I am stubborn and childish,
in the midst of this wreckage of life they incurred,
I practice being myself,
and I have found parts of myself never dreamed of by me,
they were goaded out from under rocks in my heart
when the walls were built higher,
when the water was turned off and the windows painted black.
I followed these signs
like an old tracker and followed the tracks deep into myself,
followed the blood-spotted path,
deeper into dangerous regions, and found so many parts of myself,
who taught me water is not everything,
and gave me new eyes to see through walls,
and when they spoke, sunlight came out of their mouths,
and I was laughing at me with them,
we laughed like children and made pacts to always be loyal,
who understands me when I say this is beautiful?

There's Me

There's me & Thelma & Louie & Lisa.
We're the kinda people, don't know too much about that place.
We know about factories all right, but not about how everybody
up there makes so much money.

Like Louie says, how you gonna make so much money
if you don't work? And Thelma says, sure people use their brains,
but a body works too. But a body costs a nickel, a mind costs
a million. And all them minds, what if there weren't no bodies
to work for them? Huh?

Up in that place, that's really something
uh Lisa, really something.

Here we are in clothes and talk and faces.
We know what's going on down here, but up there? Man . . .

So don't ask me why I carry a knife. Like
this, and don't ask me no questions, because I don't understand;
but take a cop wants to arrest somebody, and I'm walking
down the street, why me? He just wants to arrest somebody.
Not him, but someone told him to arrest somebody. And that
someone was told by someone else, who had little numbers in
a paper that say things ain't going too well. Now where'd
he get them numbers? Maybe from somebody with a computer
up there in one of them offices up there. Just a regular old man
or lady standing in front of a machine writing out numbers
and figuring stuff up.

Now why's he figuring something up? Ok Lisa
look: he's figuring up something, because someone else
somewhere wants him to. And you know someone who can make
him figure something up, is somebody big. Way up there . . .
probably got a whole bunch of things in this world like
boat companies and oil companies and things like that.

Just think, why does he want anyone to figure
up something? Cause one of the dudes that work for him told
him something was going wrong somewhere, and the figuring
needed to be done cuz it was messing things up.

And how does he know? I think he looks at
all these charts, you know, and if the line goes down, that
means the chump is losing. He's paid to win. So he's got
all these college dudes with degrees, thousands of them,
in a big ole building, working all day, so he can win.

They figure up everything.
   And from way up there, whatever comes out,
on a little piece of paper figured up by a thousand minds,
happens down here on the street. See what I mean?
   We're different man. You go to work Thelma
and spill coffee on tables, collect tips, smoke cigarettes,
you know, you know what's going on with yourself. And Louie
and Lisa and me, we all live, like getting good clothes,
dressing up for Friday night, riding down Central, getting
up in the morning and cursing at cockroaches, it's a good
life, better, because we know we're human beings. Know
what I mean?
   So there ain't nothing wrong with us man,
we're ok, we're good people, and our life ain't so bad man.
We'll make it, look out for each other.

New Directions Paperbooks—A Partial Listing

For complete listing request free catalog from
New Directions, 80 Eighth Avenue, New York 10011

†Bilingual

Frédéric Mistral, *The Memoirs.* NDP632.
Eugenio Montale, *It Depends.*† NDP507.
  Selected Poems.† NDP193.
Paul Morand, *Fancy Goods / Open All Night.*
  NDP567.
Vladimir Nabokov, *Nikolai Gogol.* NDP78.
  Laughter in the Dark. NDP729.
  The Real Life of Sebastian Knight. NDP432.
P. Neruda, *The Captain's Verses.*† NDP345.
  Residence on Earth.† NDP340.
New Directions in Prose & Poetry (Anthology).
  Available from #17 forward to #55.
Robert Nichols, *Arrival.* NDP437.
  Exile. NDP485.
J. F. Nims, *The Six-Cornered Snowflake.* NDP700.
Charles Olson, *Selected Writings.* NDP231.
Toby Olson, *The Life of Jesus.* NDP417.
  Seaview. NDP532.
George Oppen, *Collected Poems.* NDP418.
István Örkeny, *The Flower Show /*
  The Toth Family. NDP536.
Wilfred Owen, *Collected Poems.* NDP210.
José Emilio Pacheco, *Battles in the Desert.* NDP637.
  Selected Poems.† NDP638.
Nicanor Parra, *Antipoems: New & Selected.* NDP603.
Boris Pasternak, *Safe Conduct.* NDP77.
Kenneth Patchen, *Aflame and Afun.* NDP292.
  Because It Is. NDP83.
  Collected Poems. NDP284.
  Hallelujah Anyway. NDP219.
  Selected Poems. NDP160.
Ota Pavel, *How I Came to Know Fish.* NDP713.
Octavio Paz, *Collected Poems.* NDP719.
  Configurations.† NDP303.
  A Draft of Shadows.† NDP489.
  Selected Poems. NDP574.
  Sunstone.† NDP735.
  A Tree Within.† NDP661.
St. John Perse, *Selected Poems.*† NDP545.
J. A. Porter, *Eelgrass.* NDP438.
Ezra Pound, *ABC of Reading.* NDP89.
  Confucius. NDP285.
  Confucius to Cummings. (Anth.) NDP126.
  A Draft of XXX Cantos. NDP690.
  Elektra. NDP683.
  Guide to Kulchur. NDP257.
  Literary Essays. NDP250.
  Personae. NDP697.
  Selected Cantos. NDP304.
  Selected Poems. NDP66.
  The Spirit of Romance. NDP266.
  Translations.† (Enlarged Edition) NDP145.
Raymond Queneau, *The Blue Flowers.* NDP595.
  Exercises in Style. NDP513.
Mary de Rachewiltz, *Ezra Pound.* NDP405.
Raja Rao, *Kanthapura.* NDP224.
Herbert Read, *The Green Child.* NDP208.
P. Reverdy, *Selected Poems.*† NDP346.
Kenneth Rexroth, *An Autobiographical Novel.* NDP725.
  Classics Revisited. NDP621.
  More Classics Revisited. NDP668.
  Flower Wreath Hill. NDP724.
  100 Poems from the Chinese. NDP192.
  100 Poems from the Japanese.† NDP147.
  Selected Poems. NDP581.
  Women Poets of China. NDP528.
  Women Poets of Japan. NDP527.
Rainer Maria Rilke, *Poems from*
  The Book of Hours. NDP408.
  Possibility of Being. (Poems). NDP436.
  Where Silence Reigns. (Prose). NDP464.
Arthur Rimbaud, *Illuminations.*† NDP56.
  Season in Hell & Drunken Boat.† NDP97.
Edouard Roditi, *Delights of Turkey.* NDP445.
Jerome Rothenberg, *Khurbn.* NDP679.
  New Selected Poems. NDP625.
Nayantara Sahgal, *Rich Like Us.* NDP665.
Saigyo, *Mirror for the Moon.*† NDP465.

Ihara Saikaku, *The Life of an Amorous*
  Woman. NDP270.
St. John of the Cross, *Poems.*† NDP341.
W. Saroyan, *Madness in the Family.* NDP691.
Jean-Paul Sartre, *Nausea.* NDP82.
  The Wall (Intimacy). NDP272.
P. D. Scott, *Coming to Jakarta.* NDP672.
Delmore Schwartz, *Selected Poems.* NDP241.
  Last & Lost Poems. NDP673.
  In Dreams Begin Responsibilities. NDP454.
Shattan, *Manimekhalaï.* NDP674.
K. Shiraishi, *Seasons of Sacred Lust.* NDP453.
Stevie Smith, *Collected Poems.* NDP562.
  New Selected Poems. NDP659.
Gary Snyder, *The Back Country.* NDP249.
  The Real Work. NDP499.
  Regarding Wave. NDP306.
  Turtle Island. NDP381.
Enid Starkie, *Rimbaud.* NDP254.
Stendhal, *Three Italian Chronicles.* NDP704.
Antonio Tabucchi, *Indian Nocturne.* NDP666.
Nathaniel Tarn, *Lyrics . . . Bride of God.* NDP391.
Dylan Thomas, *Adventures in the Skin Trade.*
  NDP183.
  A Child's Christmas in Wales. NDP181.
  Collected Poems 1934-1952. NDP316.
  Collected Stories. NDP626.
  Portrait of the Artist as a Young Dog. NDP51.
  Quite Early One Morning. NDP90.
  Under Milk Wood. NDP73.
Tian Wen: A Chinese Book of Origins. NDP624.
Uwe Timm, *The Snake Tree.* NDP686.
Lionel Trilling, *E. M. Forster.* NDP189.
Tu Fu, *Selected Poems.* NDP675.
N. Tucci, *The Rain Came Last.* NDP688.
Martin Turnell, *Baudelaire.* NDP336.
Paul Valéry, *Selected Writings.*† NDP184.
Elio Vittorini, *A Vittorini Omnibus.* NDP366.
Rosmarie Waldrop, *The Reproduction of Profiles.*
  NDP649.
Robert Penn Warren, *At Heaven's Gate.* NDP588.
Vernon Watkins, *Selected Poems.* NDP221.
Eliot Weinberger, *Works on Paper.* NDP627.
Nathanael West, *Miss Lonelyhearts &*
  Day of the Locust. NDP125.
J. Wheelwright, *Collected Poems.* NDP544.
Tennessee Williams, *Baby Doll.* NDP714.
  Camino Real. NDP301.
  Cat on a Hot Tin Roof. NDP398.
  Clothes for a Summer Hotel. NDP556.
  The Glass Menagerie. NDP218.
  Hard Candy. NDP225.
  In the Winter of Cities. NDP154.
  A Lovely Sunday for Creve Coeur. NDP497.
  One Arm & Other Stories. NDP237.
  Red Devil Battery Sign. NDP650.
  A Streetcar Named Desire. NDP501.
  Sweet Bird of Youth. NDP409.
  Twenty-Seven Wagons Full of Cotton. NDP217.
  Vieux Carre. NDP482.
William Carlos Williams,
  The Autobiography. NDP223.
  The Buildup. NDP259.
  Collected Poems: Vol. I. NDP730.
  Collected Poems: Vol. II. NDP731.
  The Doctor Stories. NDP585.
  Imaginations. NDP329.
  In the American Grain. NDP53.
  In the Money. NDP240.
  Paterson. Complete. NDP152.
  Pictures from Brueghel. NDP118.
  Selected Poems (new ed.) NDP602.
  White Mule. NDP226.
Wisdom Books: *Early Buddhists.* NDP444;
  Spanish Mystics. NDP442; *St. Francis.* NDP477;
  Taoists. NDP509; *Wisdom of the Desert.* NDP295;
  Zen Masters. NDP415.

For complete listing request free catalog from
New Directions, 80 Eighth Avenue, New York 10011

†Bilingual